House Investing:

Location, Location, Location! Circumnavigate the Complex Process of Picking a Profitable Investment House

© **Copyright 2017 by _____ - All rights reserved.**

The follow eBook is reproduced below with the goal of providing information that is as accurate and reliable as possible. Regardless, purchasing this eBook can be seen as consent to the fact that both the publisher and the author of this book are in no way experts on the topics discussed within and that any recommendations or suggestions that are made herein are for entertainment purposes only. Professionals should be consulted as needed prior to undertaking any of the action endorsed herein.

This declaration is deemed fair and valid by both the American Bar Association and the Committee of Publishers Association and is legally binding throughout the United States.

Furthermore, the transmission, duplication or reproduction of any of the following work including specific information will be considered an illegal act irrespective of if it is done electronically or in print. This extends to creating a secondary or tertiary copy of the work or a recorded copy and is only allowed with express written consent from the Publisher. All additional right reserved.

The information in the following pages is broadly considered to be a truthful and accurate account of facts and as such any inattention, use or misuse of the information in question by the reader will render any resulting actions solely under their purview. There are no scenarios in which the publisher or the original author of this work can be in any fashion deemed liable for any hardship or damages that may befall them after undertaking information described herein.

Additionally, the information in the following pages is intended only for informational purposes and should thus be thought of as universal. As befitting its nature, it is presented without assurance regarding its prolonged validity or interim quality. Trademarks that are mentioned are done without written consent and can in no way be considered an endorsement from the trademark holder.

Table of Contents

Introduction 1

Chapter 1: Look with a Plan 2

Chapter 2: Finding a Rental Property 6

Chapter 3: Finding a Fix and Flip Property............................... 12

Chapter 4: Finding a Turnkey Property 19

Chapter 5: Understanding Real Estate Investment Taxes 26

Chapter 6: Negotiation 33

Conclusion... 39

Introduction

Congratulations on downloading *House Investing: Location, Location, Location! Succumb Negative the Complex Process of Picking a Profitable Investment House* and thank you for doing so. When it comes to investing in real estate successfully, knowing how to go about finding the right property, or even what the "right property" looks like is half the battle.

As such, the following chapters will discuss everything you need to know when it comes to selecting the perfect property to move forward with, regardless of what your real estate investment plans might be. First you will learn how to make a plan that will help you ensure you are on the right track when you do start looking at properties. Next, you will learn about what to look for when searching for rental real estate investments. Then you will learn about the characteristics of a great fix and flip find. From there, you will learn about how to find a reliable turnkey rental property for ultimate passive income generation.

With the property locating tips out of the way, you will then learn about the tax considerations you will need to keep in mind when looking at different types of properties. Finally, you will learn some negotiation tips to ensure that you get the best price possible on any properties you do choose to place an offer on.

There are plenty of books on this subject on the market, thanks again for choosing this one! Every effort was made to ensure it is full of as much useful information as possible, please enjoy! Even still, finding the house, finding the money to pay for it and renovating it successfully is a complicated process which is why it has been broken up into a three-part series to better discuss its intricacies effectively. The other two parts can be found here and here.

Chapter 1: Look with a Plan

Starting the process of looking for a real estate investment property is exciting, so much so, that it can be easy to jump in without taking the time to ensure you know what it is you are getting yourself into. Likewise, just because real estate investment is recommended for every investor at one point or another, doesn't mean it is right for you, right now. Making a plan, first and foremost, will help you to ensure that it is really the optimum way for you to invest in the moment. When making your plan it is important that you take a hard look at your current situation while you go over the following details.

Consider your current long-term investment plans: When it comes to determining a successful plan, the first thing you are going to need to do is to determine where you are currently at. This means going through all of your financial documents and determining exactly how much you have compared to how much you owe. This will be useful when it comes to anticipating what types of loans you get, while also helping you determine what it is that you can realistically afford.

In addition, you are going to want to consider what type of savings you have, both that you are willing to commit to putting towards a property and what you have left over in case of a rainy day. Not only is it important to have at least three months' worth of capital saved in case the worse happens while you are in the midst of getting the investment situated, this is another thing that major financial institutions are going to look for when you apply for a loan.

Consider how you are going to pay for the investment: If you already have $100,000 or so sitting around waiting for the right deal, then you can skip this step; otherwise, you will want to start by determining how much you currently have available to put down on the property. While there are a number of ways to go about getting a property with no money down (discussed in another book in this series) the easiest way to go about doing so is to ensure that you have at least 30 percent of the total amount that you are going to be asking for in a loan.

In addition to having cash on hand, the next thing you are going to need is to have a credit score that is as squeaky clean as possible. A credit score over 700 is going to see you getting an improved interest rate at a traditional financial institution with anything less than 680 being enough to start negatively impacting your end results.

If your finances aren't quite where they need to be, this doesn't mean that you can't pursue real estate investment, it just means you are going to need to work harder and more creatively in order to reach your goal. Alternatively, you may want to consider ventures that are more speculative in nature to make up the difference as well.

Consider a contingency plan: When it comes to investing in real estate successfully in the long-term, you need more than just a successful plan, you also need a reliable contingency plan in case everything goes wrong. If the property that you end up purchasing has issues that were not initially apparent, and those issues are going to make the property a non-starter, you need to know how you are going to satisfy the loan on the property without losing your shirt in the process.

If the issue was with a fix and flip, for example, perhaps you can turn it into a rental and recoup the extra costs in the long-term. If it was going to be a rental, perhaps you can wholesale the property and recoup your losses that way instead, the exact execution doesn't matter as long as you know what you are going to do if thing suddenly start imploding so you can act on the plan as quickly as possible if the worst does occur.

Consider your support system: While having a reliable support system will make it easier to get into any type of investment for the first time, it is especially crucial when it comes to real estate investment. This is due to the fact that there is such a wide variety of variables that need to be taken into account on a regular basis, many of which you likely won't be anticipating your first time out of the gate. Knowing that you have someone available to bounce ideas off of alone will make the entire process less stressful and allow you to move forward with as much confidence as possible when it comes time to close your first deal.

First and foremost, you are going to benefit a great deal from the insight and experience that a good local real estate investment club can provide. This type of organization is an invaluable resource for any new real estate investor and any city of medium size or larger will likely have a few to choose from. Barring that, an online forum with reliable posters can be a great way to get much of the same information in more remote areas though you will lose the benefit of insight on local matters.

Consider if you want to be active or passive: Real estate investment comes in two varieties and the one that you choose is going to determine the types of properties you are going to look for as well as how you will ultimately generate a profit from your investments. If you want to be an active investor then you are going to want to focus on either fix and flip properties or wholesaling properties depending on your skillset and connections. These types of real estate investments are going to be short-term and will generate all of their profits up front. They are going to have more risk, but larger actionable rewards that you can ultimately use to purchase properties that will be useful in a more passive way in the future.

Alternately, you can choose passive real estate investment options such as investing in rental properties or real estate investment trusts, which function like stocks for real estate investments. With passive real estate investments, the payout is going to come in the long-term in the form of reliable payments on a schedule you can set your watch on. These investments can be run by a third party or set up by a turnkey real estate investment company to be as passive as possible. Additionally, they can be used as a means of generating ancillary income, depending on the property type, through the use of things like paid washers and dryers.

Start an LLC: Regardless of what other plans you might have for your real estate investment future, one of the first things you are going to want to do is ensure that you start a Limited Liability Company. Doing so is quick and easy and can be done online for just a few hundred dollars. This simple action will protect your personal assets from legal action should the worst occur and someone is seriously injured while on the property. Starting an LLC makes the injury and any related legal or hospital fees the problem of the company which means that, if worse comes to worse, you can simply shutter the LLC and walk away. When it comes to protecting your profits, this should be the first step in any plan.

Chapter 2: Finding a Rental Property

For those who are taking their first steps into real estate investing, it is recommended that they start with either a single-family property or with a small multi-family property. When it comes to successfully choosing the right type of initial investment property it is important to take into account the state of the surrounding neighborhood as well as any ancillary benefits that may be nearby. It is also important to consider what other properties in the area are going for as well as what the tax rate is like in the area and surrounding neighborhoods.

Depending on the type of property that you settle on, these ideals will be of varying importance. As an example, if you purchased a single-family property in a college town then you would be confident in the fact that you will always have a steady stream of new renters in the area, though you would be limited to what you can charge based on the wide variety of other options that are likely available in the same area. It is also important to decide early if you are going to be interested in taking an active role in managing the property or if you are instead going to be more interested in generating truly passive income through the use of a property management company. Understanding how you will proceed early on will allow you to take into account any additional fees that may need to come into play while you are making your primary calculations.

Property types

Condominiums: For those who are just getting into rental real estate investment, condominiums are always a great place to start for numerous different reasons. The most important of which is that they tend to attract a low-impact renter, typically a younger professional type, who isn't going to have a hard time paying their rent and is going to be respectful of the property while also not causing trouble for the neighbors. Condominiums are also an easy way to get started as they automatically come with a property management company in place to so you can ease yourself in to all the day to day tasks if that is a direction you are interested in moving in.

On the other hand, you are going to be limited in what you can charge for rent with these properties as if you overcharge the potential tenant won't have to go far to find a better deal. Likewise, the value of your investment is going to appreciate more slowly than with other types of property, which is also why they are going to be much cheaper than the other investment types on this list. Condo renters rarely stay for the long-term, typically staying no more than then length of a lease or two and then moving on with their changing lifestyles.

Single-family homes: Renters looking for single family homes tend to be more stationary in the long-term which means it is often possible to find a renter that will stay for years, filling your pocket all the while. These types of properties typically either attract families or other social units who are commited to long-term cohabitation. This also typically makes it more likely that the rent is always going to be paid on time as there will generally be more than one person holding down a full-time job.

The biggest downside to these types of properties is that the renters can often have more complicated demands than renters who are only planning on staying in a property for a short period of time which means that you might need to put more time into the property upfront than you otherwise might. Furthermore, if it is your first rental property then you are likely going to need to do more work up front to it than you otherwise might. It may also be more difficult for you to find a property management company to work with you up front as most prefer not to work with investors of only one or two single-family homes.

Duplexes and apartments: These types of properties tend to provide stable returns in both the short and the long-term as it is unlikely that enough of your tenants are ever going to be late on the rent all at once to make it difficult for your bills to be paid. It is also very easy to find a property management company to work with in this instance as they are more likely to take on new clients who present them with attractive passive income streams.

On the downside, however, the quality of the individual renters that you end up with is largely going to be based around the quality of the tenants the previous management accepted which means you might be in for a bumpy ride to start. Additionally, of all the types of tenants, multi-family unit tenants are going to be those who are most likely to leave the unit in a poorer condition than how they found it. They are also the most likely to leave after a single term of the lease.

Other factors to keep in mind: Regardless of the type of property you end up settling on, it is important to keep in mind that you look for the areas with the greatest potential for an increase in appreciation rates along with those that have proven to have the greatest potential cash flow in the long-term. You will also need to be aware of the fact that you will often have a new rental property sit empty for at least a month while you find a new tenant and then again, each time you need to find a new tenant which means this fact needs to be added into your projected cash flow. At this point you will want to consider listings that are within your price range as well as those slightly above it as you never know what you might be able to get out of the seller by negotiating.

Taking stock of the property

When you are looking for a property to rent out, it is important to try and find a property that is a mix of value and easy renovation projects. This means nothing too expensive inside, in case the first set of renters decide to do something that decreases the value substantially. It doesn't matter if everything ends up being a little south of perfect, renters will generally be laxer about a wide number of things that would raise the ire of potential buyers. The ideal rental property will be one where you only need to update the counters in the kitchen and the cabinets in the bathroom in order to update the look significantly.

This doesn't mean that things which are dangerous or shabby should be allowed to stay, renters do still have standards after all, but it does mean that you won't need to worry about the health of long-term systems up front or the smaller finishing touches that would be required before a proper open house. Additionally, you won't need to worry about things like too few fans or light fixtures or if the color on the walls isn't the greatest, as long as these things are passable you shouldn't notice a decrease in renter interest.

If you are considering doing some remodeling, it is important to only undertake tasks whose costs you feel can be justified on a two-to-one basis when it comes to the additional premium you can add to the rent. One exception to the rule is going to be in the flooring, as replacing carpeting with either tile or wood will generate an amortized profit in the long run as these surfaces will stay usable for years to come while carpeting will have to be replaced after every single tenant moves out.

Each time you rotate tenants you will need to change the covers on the light switches as well as the outlets as these are prone to yellowing over time which can easily give the property a dirty and degraded feel that potential renters will pick up on even if they don't consciously realize they are doing so. Similarly, small improvements can go a long way. You rarely will need to replace toilets or showers, but a new $100 sink can go a long way towards revitalized a fading bathroom in short order. When it comes to the oven and refrigerator, as long as they can be cleaned to look good as new, and they function as intended, there is no reason to cart them out until you absolutely have to.

When it comes to the landscaping of your new property, you are going to want to consider the easiest way you can go about keeping it looking presentable without having to count on the tenant to do much of anything. A nice desert landscape might cost a little more up front but it will save you from having to clean things up every time a lazy tenant moves out.

When it comes to major purchases such as air conditioning units, hot water heaters and furnaces, the best bet is to always replace then when they are showing excessive signs of wear between tenants, which will allow you to take the time to find the best price on the replacement instead of prioritizing speed when it breaks down on a client. With that being said, as long as these items are in decent shape to start, you can easily put those purchases off for a year or more as opposed to factoring them into the cost of your initial purchase.

Ensuring you will make a profit

Aside from considering the changes you are going to need to make to your potential property, it is also important to never start negotiations on a rental property unless you have a good idea of what you will realistically be able to charge for rent. This means you are going to need to know what the local property tax is as well as what average rents in the area for similar properties are, so you can come up with a ballpark of what you can charge, along with what the property is going to cost you every year.

First things first, consider the price you think you can likely get the property for, assuming the negotiations end up going fine, but not great. From there, based on the average that similar properties are going for in the area you should be able to easily determine if, generally, the property can be profitable. Additionally, you will want to shoot for a rent that is roughly one percent of the total that you paid for the property. Ideally this means a $100,000 property would rent for $1,000, and $200,000 property would rent for $2,000 etc.

Assuming the rough estimate appears to be good to go, you can then consider what tier of property you believe it is. Top tier properties are those that are in the best neighborhoods, have unique amenities and generally have that special something about them that ensures they will never stay vacant for long. You can typically get away with charging a smaller percentage of the total price than you would for other types of properties, simply because they are never going to struggle to find renters.

Second tier properties will make up a majority of the properties you see. They will be in average neighborhoods and will be fine investments, but with lack the eye-catching style and flair of tier one homes. You will typically want to charge the standard one-percent per month for these properties as they are likely to end up sitting empty from time to time, though never for too terribly long.

Tier three properties are going to be those that need more work up front, and even then, they still aren't going to be anything to write home about. They are typically in less desirable or unsafe areas and will often sit empty for a prolonged period of time between occupants. While these properties are typically going to be priced at less than $100,000, you are going to want to charge more for rent, not less. A good rule of thumb for these properties is two percent month which means rent on an $80,000 home would be $1,600, a $70,000 home would rent for $1,4000 etc. To make up for the higher rental price you can compromise by being laxer when it comes to the leasing terms and who you will accept as a tenant.

Chapter 3: Finding a Fix and Flip Property

Fix and flip is the name given to properties that can be picked up for a discounted price and then rehabilitated into a property that can generate additional profit above and beyond what would have been possible before. This is often an extremely time-consuming process, and one that you certainly won't be able to take on alone. Nevertheless, if you make it out the other side successfully, there is no better way to make a profit investing in real estate.

ARV
When it comes to choosing a fix and flip property successfully, the first thing you are going to need to consider is the After Repair Value (ARV) of every property that you visit. This is the amount that you will likely be able to get the property for once it has been completely renovated. To ensure that the deal will ultimately be worth your while, you are going to want to ensure that the price of the property you find is never more than 70 percent of what the ARV will be. In addition to ensuring that you will be able to find someone to finance your deal, sticking firmly to this number means that you will make out well enough in the end to mean that you want to go through the entire crazy process again.

To determine an accurate ARV, the first thing you are going to want to do is to start with the amount that you feel you can purchase the property for before adding in what the renovations are going to cost as well as any additional costs and fees that you may need to factor in as well. In order to determine the likely value of potential repairs, the first dozen or so times you go to look at a property you are going to want to go with either a contractor or a property inspector who can help you learn what to look for. Over time, you will find that looking at an issue and determining the true cause gets easier with practice.

A few other things to keep in mind when determining your ARV include:

- When comparing the price to other prices in the area, make sure you are comparing to the price of houses that have already sold, not those that are still for sale. The more recent these numbers are, the more useful they are going to be for you. Nothing more than six months old will do, though numbers from within the last 90 days, or ideally 60 days would be best.

- If you can't find any local numbers then this should definitely be considered a warning sign. It could be that the area isn't in demand for a reason that is not readily visible, or it could mean that the prices for homes in the area are already overpriced. Regardless, it is enough to warrant a closer look at the particulars before you do anything else.

- If you are unable to find the price of any relevant local properties then you are going to want to go by square footage instead. Find a property with similar amenities to the one you are considering and then divide the price of that home by its total square footage. Take the resulting number and multiply it by the square footage of your home to get a rough estimate of a potential price. Assuming all things are equal this is a great way to come up with a workable estimate though a more accurate one to one comparison would be preferred. Additionally, it is important to keep in mind that the number of bedrooms and bathrooms matter, especially in family-centric homes. This means you are going to need to be sure to adjust up or down accordingly.

In addition to determining the value of the property accurately, here is a list of common repairs that often need to be done on fix and flip properties to give you an idea of the types of costs you will be coming up against on a regular basis.

Running toilet: If you find yourself the owner of a new property that has toilets that won't stop refilling, then it is likely due to a leaky fill valve. This is a fairly straightforward job for a competent plumber, and all it will take is the right tools, some cheap parts and about two hours. All together it will likely cost you anywhere between $50 and $200 for labor and about $20 in parts.

Slowing ceiling fan: You will likely need to replace a few of the fans in your new property, they could be burned out, the blades could be warped or they could simply be extremely out of fashion. Whatever the reason, as long as the room you are adding the fan to previously had a fan then installation should be relatively straightforward as you will already have the fan controls, light switch and required reinforced ceiling box in place. Even still, it will likely take a competent electrician over an hour, plus the cost of the new fan which means anywhere between $50 and $200 for the labor and $30 to $1,000 or more depending on the replacement fan you choose.

Broken drywall: Regardless of the quality of the property you purchase you are going to likely need to replace at least one patch of drywall and paint the results so that they look presentable. A competent painter can do the job no problem, likely charging either an hourly or a square foot rate. This can vary between $25 and $60 an hour or $2.50 to $5 per foot, including materials.

Cracked tile: Tile is difficult to chip, but odds are in the time that the tile has been in your new property you will need to replace at least a few. In order to replace the broken piece of tile, a handyman will need to remove the broken tiles, scrape out the remains of the glue from the space, glue down the new tiles and then grout them in place. Replacing a 2-foot section of tile will likely take about 2 hours of labor and will cost between $30 and $125 per hour plus materials costs of between $1 and $20 per foot.

As you can see, even the most basic of repairs that add up quick which is why it is important to take someone with you who can determine all the costs on the fly until you are able to do so yourself.

Learning to determine the true ARV of a property on the fly is crucial to your long-term real estate investment success as it will allow you to act more fluidly in the moment if you really are in the presence of a great deal. While sticking to the 70 percent rule might seem rather harsh, in addition to cutting down your pool of potential candidates significantly, it is important to nevertheless do so as moving even five percent can start to have a serious impact on your potential profits.

When it comes to deciding the price the property could potentially be worth, it is important to keep in mind the type of buyer who is most likely to be interested in the property once it is completed. This will make it easier to determine not only what they are going to be likely to pay, but also the types of renovations you should prioritize. If you are looking at properties in a rural area then you are going to want to seek out properties that have extra room for animals or recreational vehicles, along with the zoning required to make such things legal. Alternately, if you are looking in a family neighborhood then you are going to want to prioritize things like quality schools, extra bedrooms and extra bathrooms.

Regardless of the type of property that you come across, there is always going to be money to be made as long as you have a clear idea, when it comes to potential renovation plans, right from the start. Playing to the strengths of the property will not only reduce your renovation costs, it will make it easier to sell the property for a greater overall profit as well.

When it comes to considering individual renovations, it is important to consider the cost of the project along with what it is potentially going to add to the overall value of the property once things are said and done. This doesn't mean you are going to want to blindly gut every property you come across, however; and instead will want to focus on choosing potential renovations that are going to directly increase the value of the property when it is resold. This means you will want to reconsider projects such as enlarging a kitchen or living room unless the current setup is completely untenable. A project of this magnitude is going to likely cost at least $20,000 and is likely to recoup half of that. Always consider the bottom line above all else when determining what potential renovations would look like.

Don't forget to factor in the costs for decorating and painting as well, as they can add up if you don't plan for them up front. Always plan for neutral colors that are going to work well with as many different color schemes as possible. The end goal will be to create a space that potential buyers can pictures themselves in as soon as they walk in and garish or deeply personalized color choices will make this mental transference much more difficult.

Regardless of how much you like a potential property of feel personally that it would be a worthwhile investment, it is crucial to your long-term success that you never get too attached to the property. If you aren't careful you can end up emotionally invested in the property which means that you could be allowing your emotions to influence every aspect of the sale, and is a poor way to guarantee the stability of your investment. This is always going to be a poor choice because the only changes that should ever be made to the ARV once a deal has been made should be those based on the current strength of the market both local and nationwide. For the best results, keep all of the properties you work on at a healthy emotional distance.

Finally, it is important to keep in mind that a successfully fix and flip is one that happens as quickly as possible, not one that makes the owner the greatest possible amount of profit. The sooner that you finish with the first house, the sooner you can go ahead and move onto the second which means the extra month it might take to get the ultimate price you are looking for is only going to hold off the start date of your next investment. A few thousand dollars here and there to keep things rolling along as quickly as possible is a small price to pay for a well-oiled real estate investment machine.

Consider ugly duckling properties

Ugly duckling properties are properties that most investors aren't going to look twice at because they feel that they will be too much effort, regardless of the payout. These properties that have major flaws that will need to be fixed before they can be sold or rented which means they are not for everyone. While this means they won't be the right choice for everyone, it does mean that, for those who can manage them, they can be picked up for amazing deals than what would otherwise be possible. As such, while ugly duckling renovations tend to take longer, the final profit tends to be greater than with a traditional fix and flip property.

A word or warning, it is important to have reliable funding in place before you go this route as many traditional financial institutions and hard money lenders are going to have a hard time seeing your vision for these types of properties. You should also keep in mind that this type of real estate investment is typically one of the riskiest as well as there is so much can go wrong with the property that could result in it being worth less than what you were anticipating once you purchased it.

When looking for ugly duckling properties, your goal should be to look beyond what is currently there to find the potential that is hiding behind the years, or even decades of neglect. This means you are going to be more interested in the bones of the property then the superficial things that can easily be changed with a little extensive restoration and renovation. With everything that is going to be required to get these properties into a sellable state there are a few additional things you will need to keep in mind before you pursue this course of action.

First and foremost, just because you will be able to get the property for a steal, doesn't mean you likely won't need to come up with at least $60,000 to $70,000, without factoring in the costs of the renovations which are likely going to cost a fair portion of that in most instances, though often you can find a contractor who is willing to wait for payment until after the property has sold. You may be able to get credit from hardware stores and the like when it comes to materials but this will largely depend on the store, how much credit you need and what collateral you can provide.

Additionally, these types of properties regularly have hidden issues that are not revealed until ancillary work is completed which means you will likely need to budget an extra $10,000 for emergency costs if you want to get through the project without having to worry about scrambling for additional funds in the moment. All of which means you are never going to want to pay more for a property than you know you can sell it for, as is, at the drop of the hat. These types of properties naturally come with far more risk than a traditional investment which means you need to know that you are going to be able to recoup your losses, more or less, should things start showing signs of going south and not stopping until your investment is a smoking pile of rubble.

Chapter 4: Finding a Turnkey Property

A turnkey property is a property that is purchased under the guarantee, either written or implied, that the property will start generating a cash flow as soon as the contract is signed. Many even come with renters already attached. Unlike with a traditional property that you try and find for the best price possible, it is much more difficult to successfully negotiate for turnkey property as everything is ready to go as far as putting it to work is concerned.

While you won't necessarily make as much off of a turnkey property, you will find that the amount of work required to start seeing a return is much lower as well. Most turnkey properties also come with property management companies attached which means all you need to do is to worry about purchasing the property and let the company take care of the rest. In exchange for between 20 and 40 percent of the profits, the company will send you a check on a predetermined basis and you can rest easy at night knowing that your investment is being taken care of.

In order to move forward, all you need to do is choose the company that you are interested in working with, finalize an agreement with them and then wait for the profits to come to you. In general, you will want to plan on paying above market value for the property up front in addition to a negotiable cut of the profits the home generates. On the plus side, however, you can likely expect to see a profit within 30 days.

Turnkey property investment can be utilized by any investor who is looking for the most passive form of income possible, but is most commonly chosen by those who live in high density areas where buying local investment property is a much costlier proposition. These types of investors typically choose turnkey properties as a way of taking advantage of lower property costs in another part of the country while knowing that the property is being well taken care of at the same time.

One of the biggest misconceptions that many individuals have when they hear the phrase turnkey real estate investing is the assumption that every property with this label is automatically going to be a quality investment. Just because a property isn't in need of renovation or redecorating, however, doesn't mean that all of the numbers are going to add up in the way you want them too. This means you will want to apply the same level of due diligence to the property that you would any other real estate investment.

Regardless of where you and your turnkey property are located, you are going to want to visit it in person before you sign anything to ensure it is everything the company in question no doubt promised it would be. If you pursue this method without taking the time to physically see the property in question, then when it fails at a point in the future you will have no one to blame but yourself.

Choose your company carefully
Furthermore, you will need to really do your due diligence on the company you are considering as they are going to be the last line of defense between your property and the outside world. While teams are often an important part of real estate investment, nowhere is this going to be more the case than with turnkey real estate companies as they are going to have a serious effect on the overall profitability from before you even meet them.

When working with a turnkey company it is important to keep in mind that there are two primary types of transactions they are going to try and sell you on. First, you will often find that you will have the option of purchasing the property outright, in much the same way as you would with any other type of real estate transaction. This is the option you should always choose. Many turnkey real estate companies will also offer an alternative where they become your partner in an LLC which really owns the company. While this will require you to ultimately do even less work in the long run, it puts your ownership of the property into an odd state of limbo and also will make it more difficult for you to sell the property at a later date. It also leaves a potential opening for the turnkey company to pull something shady and should never be agreed to under normal circumstances.

While investing in a thoroughly vetted turnkey company is one of the most reliable types of real estate investment imaginable, that doesn't mean it doesn't come with the same inherent risks that any other type of real estate investment does. As with any investment, if you want to know if investing in turnkey real estate is right for you, all you need to do is consider the potential profit and then determine if that justifies the related risk in your eyes and then act accordingly.

When it comes to choosing the right turnkey property company, the first thing you are going to need to do is narrow down the potential choices as there are more than a thousand companies that offer these services across the US alone. The first thing you are going to want to do is check to see if the companies you are considering have a physical address. If you end up going through with a deal that doesn't work out as you were promised then you need to have some place you can physically go and complain. Likewise, the physical address needs to be an office, not just a PO box. If the company has an actual office, which you will see when you visit the property, then you know they are not just a fly by night operation and are going to be more likely to result in a long-term business relationship that is beneficial to everyone.

With the online operations out of the way, the next thing you will need to be aware of is recommendations from investors who have seen success with a turnkey company in the past. The best place to go for this type of information is going to be a local real estate investment club, though a recent online recommendation can also be effective as long as you have reason to trust the source. Personal recommendations are worth their weight in gold, but that doesn't mean you still won't need to personally look into the company to ensure that they remain on the level.

If you are looking for a turnkey company in another area, researching local real estate investment clubs is a great place to start. While they might not be as open as they would be with someone local, they will still likely be able to point you in the right direction if nothing else. Baring recommendations, your next best bet is going to be seeking out companies that are locally owned and operated as there are going to be fewer layers of management that you are going to need to worry about being on the level.

Once you have tracked down a few likely candidates, the next thing you are going to want to do is to read the reviews the company has received on their website and on other popular review aggregate sites. When skimming through reviews, a number of negative reviews here and there are going to be expected, and shouldn't be seen as a reason to avoid the company all together. However, this doesn't mean they should be disregarded entirely as they can provide clues to the overall quality of the service if they all complain about the same things. Never forget, forewarned is forearmed.

In addition to negative patterns, you are also going to want to ensure that the companies you are seriously considering all have a few basics under their belts to start. First, you will want to ensure that the company has been in business for at least 10 years, anything less than that and you can't guarantee that they have worked all of the kinks out of the operation yet. There is nothing to say that anything about these properties are going to be inferior, just that the companies that own them might not have hit on the best path to long-term success which means they are still experimenting. As you are investing in turn key rental properties for their stalwart and reliable nature, it's not the sort of investment that you want other people to be experimenting with.

You will also need to make sure that their renovation and management practices are easy to find and are something you can agree with. On each website, you are also going to find lots and lots of data on the local market. All of this data can be easily verified by third parties, and you are going to want to verify all of it yourself before you talk to anybody. Not only will this help to ensure that the company you choose is honest, it will also help you with the next step when it comes to ensuring that the employees are knowledgeable.

Assuming you were able to find a few companies that were able to measure up, the next step is going to be talking to representatives of the company in person to get an idea of what they are really like. First things first, when you call, if you don't hear back within 24 hours then you are going to want to look elsewhere. If they can't be bothered to contact a potential client within that time, assuming it's a business day, then how can you expect them to treat your calls once they already have your money.

Either the company does not have the resources, or the drive, to get back in touch with you and neither of these are qualities you want in the company that is going to be in charge of maximize your investment. Along those same lines, the more ways the company gives for you to easily get in touch with them, the more likely they are to actually treat your communication with respect once it is received.

When you speak with them you are also going to want to take note of the level of professionalism that they present as, again, this will reflect on the way that they are going to treat those who are potentially interested in renting from them as well. Additionally, their level of professionalism on the phone will translate to other aspects of the company which means they are going to be more likely to be worth your time than those whose employees feel it is acceptable to answer the phone in a slovenly fashion.

Furthermore, you are going to want to ensure that you can get a hold of the person who is going to be directly overseeing your property at all times, day or night. Additionally, it is important to speak with this person multiple times about problems either real or imagined. When doing so, take the time to extend the conversation long enough for you to really know if you have that person's ear or if they are just humoring you.

When speaking with the people in charge it is important to take the information you have learned about the area and determine if they have an accurate and up to date view of the market both on a micro and macro level. If you find an issue between what they are saying, press them on it; there is a good chance they might have more up to date information than you do, but if not then you will know you can cut them from your list.

When choosing which companies to reach out to, you should be able to rely on more than just your own observations, you should also be able to rely on the validation of current customers. If you weren't able to track down any recommendations at the start, make sure you ask to see current references and call as many as you need to in order to be sure about your future investment. If a company is unable or unwilling to provide a list of contacts you are going to want to take a long hard look at why this may be the case. Regardless of the answer, odds are you are going to want to look elsewhere.

It is also vital that you determine the level of support once you have given them your money as well. Even if the representation of the company in question has been extremely attentive thus far, there is nothing guaranteeing that they are going to keep that level of service moving forward. What's more, you will need to ensure that the company you are working with is going to be the company in charge of handling the day to day as this is not always going to be the case. It should go without saying that if this is not the case you will need to provide the same level of diligence on the actual property management company.

Finally, while it is correct to assume that you are going to be paying a premium for a turnkey property, that doesn't mean you still shouldn't shop around to find the best price possible and stretch your investment dollar as far as it will go. However, when looking for bargains it is important to not get suckered in by turnkey companies that have significantly lower than average prices. If you do, you will likely find yourself paying much more than you were initially expecting and often sooner rather than later. When doing your research, you should end up with a clear idea of what property in your chosen area goes for, and if you see a property that is going for less than that you should consider it a red flag.

Assuming the company knows the prices for the area in question, then there must be some other reasons for them to feel the need to price their property for lower than the market average. That reason might be something major or it might be something minor and if there is one reason that they tell you about, there are likely two more that the won't which mean it is best to leave that particular can of worms unopened, regardless of how badly you may want to see what's inside.

Chapter 5: Understanding Real Estate Investment Taxes

In order to truly profit from real estate investment in the long-term, the first thing you need to understand is the difference between real estate business and real estate investments. Real estate business is anything that is short-term and real estate based such as a fix and flip or a property wholesale. A real estate investment is primarily rental property or investments made in REITs. Depending on your personal situation you are going to want to start with one and then move into the other, or possibly just start with rental investments right out of the gate. Regardless of the way you go, however, it will be helpful to understand the tax ramifications of your choices.

In order to need to pay taxes, the first thing you are going to need to do is to make money through your investment property which can be done in several different ways. In order to remember them all, just think of real estate as an IDEAL investment.

Income: The I in IDEAL represents any regular profits that are generated from the property such as interest or rent payments. While somewhere between five and 10 percent is going to be seen as average for this type of return, with practice, and a little extra hard work, you can easily get it as high as 15 percent.

Depreciation: The D in IDEAL represents an accounting method applied to real estate that amortizes the cost out over a set period of time, different assets depreciate at different rates and real estate depreciates over 27.5 years. This fact will be discussed more later but it can essentially be used to offset other taxes that you pay at the end of the year.

Equity: The E in IDEAL represents the most efficient way to pay off rental properties which is to charge more than you are required to pay for the mortgage each month in rent and then put the full amount towards paying off the property. This will ensure that you are paying off more than just the interest each month which means that the amount of principal that is being paid then gets bigger and bigger as the rental amount will always stay the same (equity). It works the same way that compounding does on a savings account with the amount being paid towards the principle acting as the compounding interest.

Appreciation: The A in IDEAL represents the amount that the property will naturally increase in value over time based on external factors. While most appreciation is passive, you can generate active appreciation by continuing to work on the property over time, raising the appreciation value as you go.

Leverage: The L in IDEAL represents any debt that you may have taken on in order to purchase the property. Taking on debt is essentially leveraging the money that you do have to ensure that you can generate the maximum return on your investment dollar. For example, if you had $100,000 investment capital on hand, it would make more sense to finance four separate loans with $25,000 down on each as opposed to buying one property for $100,000 cash.

You are going to want to be on the lookout for these types of profit centers for every potential property that you come across. Be aware that you are unlikely to see all of them in the same property and you may well need to decide which you need to prioritize as you may need to give up one to get another.

Real estate tax benefits

Depreciation: The IRS understands that assets wear eventually wear out and become less valuable. While this isn't true when it comes to most real estate, the asset classifications works out in your favor and you receive a 27.5 year depreciation rate for each property that you purchase. Unlike other expenses for your real estate ventures, depreciation is what is known as a paper loss which means you aren't actually required to spend any money in order to claim it. This expense can then be used to offset taxable income and save you money on your tax bill.

For example, say you had $5,000 in taxable rental income and a federal tax rate of 25 percent. This would mean you owed $1,250 in taxes before depreciation. When it is factor in, however, you get $3,000 worth of depreciation expenses taken out of the $5,000 worth of rental income so the taxes are taken from $2,000 for a total of $500. This is especially useful as there is no ceiling on its effectiveness, the higher the tax rate on the property, the more you end up saving.

While depreciation is not unique to real estate, this type of investing benefits more so than other instances as the cost of real estate is substantial and frequently purchased via leverage. For example, a property that is worth $200,000, depreciated regularly, will generate a savings in taxes of nearly $7,500 each year. If you then had three properties worth this amount you would be sheltering more than $20,000 worth of income and see as much as $5,500 back on your taxes, assuming you were taxed at a rate of 25 percent.

It is also worthwhile to keep in mind that while the IRS is generous when it comes to purchasing and holding properties, it is equally stingy when it comes time to eventually sell. This means that when you prepare to sell a property you will need to recapture the depreciated amount at the rate of 25 percent. This means you are going to end up with serious incentives to keep the property for the long-term or use alternative savings strategies to get around this steep cost.

Unfortunately, there are some limits when it comes to depreciation. Prior to 1986 this was not the case and investors could take full advantage of the full amount of shelter that a given property provided. Some investors even bought properties specifically for their tax advantages. The IRS wasn't a fan of this system so they changed the rules and now things don't work the same way in the event of a significant loss. For example, if you make $3,000 from renting out a property and have a depreciation expense of $5,000 then you are left with a passive loss of $2,000 which cannot be used as a shelter. This is not the case if you are claiming the difference the year you sell the property or if you are a licensed real estate professional. You can also still use a deduction of as much as $25,000 if you make less than $100,000 in a year and you are not using a turnkey rental property service.

Avoid FICA: Income from rental properties is not going to be subject to taxes that relate to either Medicare or social security, though income from a fix and flip would. While this might not sound like much at first, it is significant over an extended period of time as most other income is taxed at nearly eight percent for these privileges. If you are self-employed that rate jumps to more than 15 percent. However, if you earn $100,000 worth of rental income during that same year then that money will go into your pocket tax free. When you consider how much that 15 percent could add up in a savings account over a 30-year depreciation span that extra money starts looking pretty good.

Appreciation: Like rental income, the appreciation that occurs with a property while you hold it is not taxed. This fact is a large part of what has led to Warren Buffet's success and he is fond of saying that his favorite length of time to hold a property for is forever. If you eventually sell then you are going to be required to pay taxes, commissions and transaction fees which will all hurt your long-term profits as you lose out on the ability of every dollar spent to grow and increase in value over time. As these profits aren't taxed, it is possible to let your net worth grow significantly without exposing yourself to any additional tax risk.

Lower rates for capital gains: Capital gains are the amount that you make on the profit of the sale of a property. The amount you make in the year that you sell the property is going to determine how much you have to pay in capital gains taxes. In the short-term you will have to pay 25 percent if you make between $37,951 and $91,900 in a given year, 28 percent if you make up to $191,650 in a given year, 33 percent if you make up to $416,700 in a given year, 35 percent if you make up to $418,400 and 39.6 percent if you make more than that. In long-term taxes you will need to pay 15 percent if you make between $37,951 and $418,400 and 20 percent if you make more than that. Even if you manage to hit the 20 percent long-term capital gains tax bracket you will still be paying less than what you would for a comparable amount of traditional income taxes.

Avoid all taxes: If you wish to completely avoid having to deal with capital gains taxes on a fix and flip property then all you need to do is to declare the property as your primary residence while you are completing the fix and flip. Before you start thinking about defrauding the federal government, they will be out to check and make sure you are actually living in the property on a full-time basis. If you plan on remodeling the property by yourself, then you will likely need at least two years which is the minimum amount of time you will need to live in the property in order to claim a maximum of $250,000 in profit for yourself of $500,000 for you and a partner.

Exchanging properties: Another useful way to avoid paying a capital gains tax, along with any required depreciation recaptures is what is known as a 1031 tax-free exchange. Named after US tax code section 1031, this technique allows you to trade properties with someone else, thus allowing you to both defer paying taxes on your new properties until you eventually sell them.

As previously mentioned, any time you can defer paying taxes is money that you can put to use investing to ensure that it grows to far more than what you would have ended up with if you had paid the taxes in the first place. As an example, if you sell a property for $300,000 and pay a total of $35,000 in recapture and depreciation taxes. If you invested that $35,000 for 20 years and saw a 10 percent return on your investment you would have an extra $235,000 and that is from just one property.

Installment sales: The IRS also provides investors with another tool when it comes to minimizing the amount they pay in taxes on completed real estate transactions. Known as the seller carry-back or installment sale, this type of transactions is only available to investors, not those who make their living selling houses. This method also allows you to defer any depreciation recaptures, though the full amount will need to be paid back in the event of an ultimate sale.

Essentially, an installment sale just means that the seller will receive their payments in small amounts over a set length of time rather than all at once. The seller is then essentially giving the buyer credit to purchase the property, similar to owner-financing. As an example, the owner of duplex could sell a $300,000 property for $30,000 down and $2,000 a month for

20 years at an interest rate of six percent. If the current owner purchased the property for just $50,000 at a point in the past then an installment sale would mean they only need to pay taxes on the profit from the sale they received in a given year. While a $250,000 windfall might push the seller into a higher tax bracket, hurting total profits, the slow and steady payments will work out to cost less in the long run. This is also a viable strategy for those who have been actively management properties and are looking for a way to transition into a more passive income stream.

Borrow tax-free: A common way that many investors raise cash for upcoming investments is to sell existing investments. Unfortunately, this process exposes you to a variety of complicated procedures and potential tax repayments. There is another way, however, you can also pull capital out of an existing investment, without paying any taxes by refinancing.

When compared to straight up selling, refinancing can have numerous different benefits including allowing you to hold onto an investment that is already performing as anticipated or better. It can also help you benefit from loan amortization as your tenants will help you pay off the loan. You will also see a benefit in terms of additional appreciation the property will see while you continue to hold it. Finally, you won't have to pay any taxes on the money you have acquired as it is borrowed.

While this process will certainly open you up to additional debt, especially if the existing property or the new property isn't a sure thing, this can be said about any new investment opportunity as well. As long as you have done your homework and are sure that the new debt looks attractive, if it has long amortization, low rates or fixed interest for example, or if it is covered conservatively with cash reserves or cash flow then you might want to consider the risks and benefits in your specific situation.

Self-directed IRA: 401ks and IRAs are both extremely useful tools when it comes to building wealth in the long-term while also actively working to minimize your taxes. While most people don't think of them when it comes to real estate investments, this can be a costly mistake as the IRS does not dictate what an IRA can invest in, only what is not allowed and real estate is definitely not on the disapproved list.

While a self-directed IRA can be an extremely useful tool, there are plenty of rules to follow and pitfalls to avoid. What's more, if you accidentally break a rule, even if you weren't aware of it at the time, you can be subject to a hefty fine which can cut into your overall profits in a hurry which mean you are likely best going with something more directed, at least at first.

One of the most useful ways of investing in real estate via an IRA is through the loan you take out to purchase the property in the first place. Going through the process in this fashion ensures lower overall risk and fewer overall moving parts than actually owning the real estate itself.

Chapter 6: Negotiation

The golden rule in real estate is that everything is negotiable, and this is true, up to a point. When you are buying your first real estate investment property you are going to naturally want to get the best deal that you can to maximize your future profits, this doesn't mean you need to haggle over ever last red cent, however, and sometimes knowing when to stop is as important as knowing when to go full bore.

The best way to learn the limits starts with knowing the area surrounding the property as thoroughly as possible, down to the neighborhood and street if possible. First things first, if there are more homes for sale in the area than the local average then this means you are lucky enough to find yourself in a buyer's market. This means you are going to be able to make more demands, and even take an extra 10 percent off any offers that you make. If the alternative is true then you are looking at a seller's market which means that you are going to be lucky to pay the asking price and might need to make a few more concessions than you otherwise would.

With so many home listings available online, it can be easy to see the logic in trying to save some extra money by not using a real estate agent during your real estate investment endeavors. It is more difficult than you might expect to get a property successfully from offer to close, however, and there is a lot you can learn from a good real estate agent that makes them worthwhile your first few times out at least. A good agent will also have negotiation experience and insider details about the market that can pull a successful deal together from almost nothing. What's more, as the buyer, you won't be paying for the agent, that will be covered in a commission paid by the seller.

Ways to ensure a successful negotiation

Be quick: You never know how long a counteroffer is going to remain on the table or what other deals might be taking place behind the scenes on the off chance that yours falls through. As such, you are always going to want to respond as quickly as possible and ensure that you don't die on any hills related to terms that aren't actually deal breakers. Everyone likes to win but if you hope to be successful in real estate investment then you are going to have to learn to pick your battles.

Any delays in your response gives the seller the opportunity to think about the fact that other deals are out there or for additional buyers to step in and try to create a bidding war. This is the absolute last thing you want to happen as if a seller even gets an idea that there might be a bidding war then your smooth transaction is likely to get a whole lot more complicated.

Use the proper channels: When you are negotiating, it is important to never attempt to contact the seller directly and to instead always go through your real estate agent for all relevant communications. While this might seem unprofessional or timid, going against the norm will make you look unprofessional and pushy and will do nothing to improve your overall odds of success.

What's more, many of the ins and outs of real estate negotiation are tricky to master and require precise wording in order to ensure you get what you want out of the situation. Going through the proper channels will ensure that your needs are communicated adequately while also guaranteeing that the deal you end up signing contains the details you anticipate, not those the other party was able to trick you into signing due to poor word choice.

Ensure you have the best info possible: If you can find up to date information on sales that were recently completed, the next best thing is going to be a list of properties that are currently pending. While this information isn't always going to be available, you will find that you can often talk to the real estate agents in question who will be sympathetic if you explain to them your current situation. At the very least you will often find that your real estate agent can call them up and, through professional courtesy, at least get a reasonable estimate for what the property is selling for.

While it is important to take full advantage of your real estate agent, it is also important to ensure that you look up the price of any comparable properties yourself rather than trusting your real estate agent to provide you with the true prices. The reason for this is that the agent will get a cut of the total sales price which means it is in their best interest to get the most for the property possible. Don't get lulled into using a false price floor, do your own research, your wallet will thank you. You will also want to be sure to ask for a copy of the comparative market analysis along with the full MLS listings on the related properties so you can see just how similar they really are.

Ensure your agent works for their money: When you are competing with other real estate investors to ensure that you get the best deal you are going to want to ensure that you have every advantage possible. In these instances, the work that your real estate agent does when it comes to presentation and preparation can make the difference between success and failure. Ideally you will have put time and effort into selecting the best real estate agent available which means they are going to be willing to go the extra mile when it counts. Use this fact to your advantage and make them work for their commission. Ensure you always communicate clearly with your agent to keep you both on the same page when it comes to potential deal breakers or other expectations.

Know the numbers: Before you can successfully offer up a number to start the negotiations, you are going to need to know exactly what you can afford, after factoring in insurance, taxes and the cost of the property itself. It is important to know exactly what this means you will be paying each month, and have a clear idea of how much room for variance that you have before the negotiation starts. As the search for the right profitable property creeps on, it is common for the price the buyer is comfortable with paying to inch its way upwards. It is important to avoid this temptation and stick to your guns in order to ensure the property that you end up with can actually end up turning a profit for you when everything is said and done.

If you are having a tough time determining the right price to offer, running the numbers of a few different prices can have surprisingly different results. When you run the payment, insurance and tax information you will be surprised at how much of an impact just $5,000 or $10,000 can have on the long-term price of a given property and can make the decision about what to offer much clearer than it would otherwise have been.

Set your offer the right way: When it comes to making an offer on a property, it is important to always set your own price based on what the home is worth, assuming it is not significantly undervalued. If this is the case then the other person's mistake should definitely be your gain and you shouldn't feel obligated to pay more than they are offering because they didn't do enough research. Likewise, if it is priced above market value, feel free to base your offer on what the property is really worth. Unless they know something you don't, the seller is likely just trying to get lucky and will still take any reasonably priced offers seriously.

Don't count on the final inspection for additional negotiations: While you will always have the right to ask for a credit if the final inspection reveals anything major, that doesn't mean you are going to get it. These days it is extremely unlikely for the seller to be willing to reopen negotiations, or be willing to make significant additional repairs to a property, which means you need to be aware of these problems as soon as possible so you can ask for a credit at closing so that you can find a contractor after the fact who is able to work with a very specific budget. You are always going to want to do your inspection during the initial walkthrough to ensure that you don't have to worry about getting in contact with the listing agent more than you absolutely have to. Remember, any delay at this stage is an opportunity to steal your good deal out from under you.

Never be afraid to ask: Regardless of the market, you should always ask for every repair, minor or otherwise, along with any addition concessions, as long as you understand that you won't get them all. However, once you are in escrow, the balance of power will shift in your favor, regardless of the current market, as no seller wants to end up back at square one with a property back on the market after all the work has been done to get it to a point where it is almost sold. The time when you have the greatest amount of power is going to be when the inspection period has just about ended. When it comes to getting what you ask for, just remember that what you get in return for a concession the seller can't make will always be more than what you would have gotten if you kept your mouth shut.

Know everything you can about the seller: Personal details about the seller's life can often be used to your advantage, but only if you press the real estate agent for them before you appear to be interested or go ahead and make an offer. At that point, any information they give out is giving information to the other side and will be practically impossible to come by in many instances. If you ask early and often, however, then you are just making conversation.

If you know the seller has already found a new home, for example, then you can reasonably assume that they are looking to get things finished as quickly as possible and you can tailor the offer accordingly. Likewise, if they haven't yet found a new property then they might be amenable to an agreement where they pay you rent on the property for a few months up front. Either way, you never would have even known about the potential without doing your homework up front.

Understand that compromise will occur: Regardless of how good you are at negotiations, there is no way that you are going to go into a real estate negotiation and come out with everything you want, it just isn't going to happen. Going in with an all or nothing mindset is reductive and will only end up causing the negotiation to stall or with you ending up with a subpar deal because you weren't willing to make concessions you didn't care about in exchange for things that you did.

Before going into any negotiation, you are going to want to know exactly what you can't live without from the upcoming negotiation, the things you would like to have but can live without in small numbers and the things you don't really care about that you will use as bargaining chips for the things that matter most. Likewise, you are going to need to know your ideal number, a number you can live with and a number you will have to walk away from. Having all of this information in mind from the start will allow you to act more confidently throughout the negotiation process.

Conclusion

Thank you for making it through to the end of *House Investing: Location, Location, Location! Succumb Negative the Complex Process of Picking a Profitable Investment House*, let's hope it was informative and able to provide you with all of the tools you need to achieve your goals, whatever it is that they may be. Just because you've finished this book doesn't mean there is nothing left to learn on the topic, expanding your horizons is the only way to find the mastery you seek.

The best real estate investors are those who are the ones that keep their ear to the ground when it comes to new avenues for lead generation and changing buyer or renter trends which means they cultivate the habit of lifelong learning as early as possible. Failing to do so is akin to leaving money on the table. Even still, finding the house, finding the money to pay for it and renovating it successfully is a complicated process which is why it has been broken up into a three-part series to better discuss its intricacies effectively. The other two parts can be found here and here.

Getting ready to pick out your first investment property is akin to getting ready to start out on a great adventure. No great adventure that ends profitably is over quickly, however, which means that before you get started down the path of real estate investment you need to be ready to commit to the long haul. Successfully investing in real estate is a marathon, not a sprint, slow and steady wins the race.

Finally, if you found this book useful in anyway, a review on Amazon is always appreciated!

Description

When it comes to investing in real estate successfully, knowing how to go about finding the right property, or even what the "right property" looks like is half the battle. If you are interested in real estate investment but aren't sure where to start, *House Investing: Location, Location, Location! Succumb Negative the Complex Process of Picking a Profitable Investment House* is the book you have been waiting for.

Inside you will find everything you need to get started searching through the thousands and thousands of properties that are waiting right now for the right person, with the right vision, to come along and make the right deal that will turn it into a keystone of a real estate investment portfolio. You will learn how to determine if a real estate investment is going to make a reliable passive income stream via rental property or if it would be better off being renovated and sold for a huge profit a few months down the line. The possibilities are endless, you just need to know what to look for when it comes to making a good deal.

Real estate investment is one of the oldest forms of investment, and with good reason as it generates a better than average return, more reliably than any other type of investment. So, what are you waiting for? Take control of your financial future and buy this book today!

Finding the house, finding the money to pay for it and renovating it successfully is a complicated process which is why it has been broken up into a three-part series to better discuss its intricacies effectively. The other two parts can be found here and here.

Inside you will find
- Financial considerations to keep in mind to ensure you are looking for property within your means.
- The best type of rental properties to consider when you are just starting out.

- Tips for eyeballing the cost of renovations and repairs of all types on the fly.
- Secretes to getting the best price for every property, every time.
- ***And more...***

www.ingramcontent.com/pod-product-compliance
Lightning Source LLC
Chambersburg PA
CBHW050029230526
45470CB00003B/1187